Send an email to "**info@trafficjamming.com**" and write in the subject line, "Promo Code" – by doing so, this will allow you to join the TraffficJamming Business Family and receive a one-hour consultation on how to grow your customer base. In addition, you will also receive a Free Online Directory Report outlining what your prospects and clients see when searching for your business online (a $197.00 value). To learn more, visit **www.trafficjamming.com**.

Jeff Shavitz on Networking

Get Connected

By Jeff Shavitz

An Actionable Business Journal

E-mail: info@thinkaha.com
20660 Stevens Creek Blvd., Suite 210
Cupertino, CA 95014

Copyright © 2016, Jeff Shavitz

All rights reserved. No part of this book shall be reproduced, stored in a retrieval system, or transmitted by any means electronic, mechanical, photocopying, recording, or otherwise without written permission from the publisher.

> ⇨ Please pick up a copy of this book in the Aha Amplifier and share each AhaMessage socially at http://aha.pub/jeffshavitznetworking

Published by THiNKaha®
20660 Stevens Creek Blvd., Suite 210, Cupertino, CA 95014
http://thinkaha.com
E-mail: info@thinkaha.com

First Printing: February 2016
Paperback ISBN: 978-1-61699-168-5 (1-61699-168-2)
eBook ISBN: 978-1-61699-169-2 (1-61699-169-0)
Place of Publication: Silicon Valley, California, USA
Paperback Library of Congress Number: 2015953623

Trademarks

All terms mentioned in this book that are known to be trademarks or service marks have been appropriately capitalized. Neither THiNKaha, nor any of its imprints, can attest to the accuracy of this information. Use of a term in this book should not be regarded as affecting the validity of any trademark or service mark.

Warning and Disclaimer

Every effort has been made to make this book as complete and as accurate as possible. The information provided is on an "as is" basis. The author(s), publisher, and their agents assume no responsibility for errors or omissions. Nor do they assume liability or responsibility to any person or entity with respect to any loss or damages arising from the use of information contained herein.

How to Read a THiNKaha® Book
A Note from the Publisher

The THiNKaha series is the CliffsNotes of the 21st century. The value of these books is that they are contextual in nature. Although the actual words won't change, their meaning will change every time you read one as your context will change. Experience your own "aha!" moments ("AhaMessages™") with a THiNKaha book; AhaMessages are looked at as "actionable" moments—think of a specific project you're working on, an event, a sales deal, a personal issue, etc. and see how the AhaMessages in this book can inspire your own AhaMessages, something that you can specifically act on. Here's how to read one of these books and have it work for you.

1. Read a THiNKaha book (these slim and handy books should only take about 15-20 minutes of your time!) and write down one to three actionable items you thought of while reading it. Each journal-style THiNKaha book is equipped with space for you to write down your notes and thoughts underneath each AhaMessage.
2. Mark your calendar to re-read this book again in 30 days.
3. Repeat step #1 and write down one to three more AhaMessages that grab you this time. I guarantee that they will be different than the first time. BTW: this is also a great time to reflect on the actions taken from the last set of AhaMessages you wrote down.

After reading a THiNKaha book, writing down your AhaMessages, re-reading it, and writing down more AhaMessages, you'll begin to see how these books contextually apply to you. THiNKaha books advocate for continuous, lifelong learning. They will help you transform your ahas into actionable items with tangible results until you no longer have to say "aha!" to these moments—they'll become part of your daily practice as you continue to grow and learn.

As the Chief Instigator of Ahas at THiNKaha, I definitely practice what I preach. I read *Alexisms* and *Ted Rubin on How to Look People in the Eye Digitally*, and one new book once a month and take away two to three different action items from each of them every time. Please e-mail me your ahas today!

Mitchell Levy
publisher@thinkaha.com

Dedication

Dedicated to all those who recognize that developing genuine and authentic relationships builds successful businesses. It works!

Contents

Section I
On Relationship Building — 9

Section II
Get Involved — 17

Section III
Authentic Relationships Matter — 31

Section IV
Get Connected — 45

Section V
Keep in Mind — 59

Section VI
Your RoadMap to Success — 87

About the Author — 113

Section I: On Relationship Building

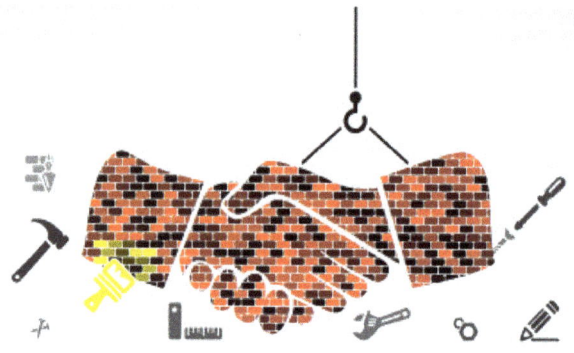

Section 1

On Relationship Building

How would you define the word "networking"? Do you really understand the importance of it? When done properly, it is one of the most powerful strategies you can use to grow your business.

Section I: On Relationship Building

1

Effective business is about networking. Do it right and you may succeed. Do it wrong and you will fail. @JeffShavitz

2

Networking isn't like reading a financial statement, where the ROI is the overriding concern in the transaction. @JeffShavitz

3

Networking involves "return on time" (ROT). Are you using your time effectively? @JeffShavitz

4

Understand the difference between ROI (Return on Investment) and ROT (Return on Time). Do you? @JeffShavitz

Section I: On Relationship Building

5

Networking is part of business. Read "Jeff Shavitz on Small Business--AhaMessages." http://aha.pub/smallbizahas @JeffShavitz

_____
_____
_____

6

Quid pro quo is the quintessential term that describes networking. Is this part of your vocabulary? @JeffShavitz

_____
_____
_____

7

Networking is a two-way street! Is it one-way or two-way for you? @JeffShavitz

_____
_____
_____

Section I: On Relationship Building

8

Networking is not a one-time exercise. The more you do it, the more you will be rewarded for it. @JeffShavitz

_____
_____
_____

9

Networking is like eating carbohydrates; the more you do it, the more you crave it.
@JeffShavitz

_____

_____

_____

10

I define networking as relationship-building. How do you define it? @JeffShavitz

_____

_____

_____

Section II: Get Involved

Section II

Get Involved

Networking isn't like reading a financial statement where the return on investment (ROI) is the primary issue. Networking involves a return on time (ROT). YOU matter! YOUR contacts matter! RECIPROCITY matters! Make time to meet others and grow your circle of business relationships and friendships.

Section II: Get Involved

11

Write an Aha Book to spotlight your expertise on a specific business issue!
http://www.ahaamplifier.com/aha/publish
@JeffShavitz

12

Seize the opportunity to speak publicly whenever you have the chance in order to build up your brand. @JeffShavitz

_____

_____

_____

13

Participating in charities and fundraisers is an excellent way to meet quality people. @JeffShavitz

_____

_____

_____

Section II: Get Involved

14

Attend at least six conferences, trade-shows, or networking events per year. @JeffShavitz

_____

_____

_____

15

Don't attend a networking event and only talk with the one person you already knew from your past. @JeffShavitz

16

Meeting one new person each week = 52 new people a year. After 10 years, you'll have 520 new business contacts. @JeffShavitz

Section II: Get Involved

17

Join a networking group with people totally "NOT" like you. I promise you that it works. Expand your relationships. @JeffShavitz

_____

_____

_____

18

Be consistent in attending networking meetings. If they are scheduled for every month, attend at least 80% of them.
@JeffShavitz

_____
_____
_____

Section II: Get Involved

19

There are plenty of customers out there for all of us to make a living. Join industry networking groups to learn. @JeffShavitz

20

Learn to play golf--a great way to spend 4 hours of quality time with a new friend / customer / vendor. @JeffShavitz

21

Be prepared in networking groups to help those who help you. @JeffShavitz

22

Evaluate the cost and time to join a membership group. Determine the potential you can and should realize. @JeffShavitz

Section II: Get Involved

23

There are many networking groups to join. Choose wisely & be as specific as possible to align business interests. @JeffShavitz

24

"Less is more"--find quality contacts through your networking efforts. @JeffShavitz

25

Accountants and lawyers are a great way to connect with other business owners.
@JeffShavitz

_____
_____
_____

26

Write down a goal for 90 days from today: Whom do you want to meet? Be targeted. Make sure you meet them! @JeffShavitz

_____

_____

_____

27

There are 15 business meals in a week (breakfast, lunch & dinner). Use this time wisely to meet with key people. @JeffShavitz

_____

_____

_____

28

Get involved in your local chamber of commerce--it's a great way to connect with people within your community. @JeffShavitz

29

Volunteering is a great way to meet influential people within your community and/or industry. @JeffShavitz

Section III: Authentic Relationships Matter

Section III

Authentic Relationships Matter

Everyone has the need to be accepted, respected, and valued. Live by "The Golden Rule." Developing trusted, authentic relationships and business partnerships takes time – but once you do, you may also be developing friendships for life.

Section III: Authentic Relationships Matter

30

Simple math: meet 100 people and each of these 100 people will know another 100 people--you now know 10,000 people. @JeffShavitz

31

Favors are a common ingredient in networking; don't be selfish, return the favors. @JeffShavitz

32

For relationships to grow, people have to first become genuinely comfortable with you. It doesn't happen overnight. @JeffShavitz

33

Once a person is comfortable with you and your services, their entire network of people will be opened up to you. @JeffShavitz

Section III: Authentic Relationships Matter

34

Doesn't everyone think they have the best doctor? Share your resources with those you meet and care about. @JeffShavitz

_____

_____

_____

35

Be nice to everyone you meet--you never know how they can help you in the future.
@JeffShavitz

_____
_____
_____

Section III: Authentic Relationships Matter

36

Tell everyone in your family and extended family what you do for a living--they can help connect you with others. @JeffShavitz

_____

_____

_____

37

Review your high school and college yearbook and reconnect with key people for mutual benefit. You have a shared bond. @JeffShavitz

_____

_____

_____

38

Share your business aspirations with your children as they become your voice with their peers & teachers. @JeffShavitz

Section III: Authentic Relationships Matter

39

Be respectful of cold-callers & spend the extra 30 seconds on the phone--they could become a lead for you. @JeffShavitz

_____
_____
_____

40

Get involved with your local community--it's the right thing to do from a civic responsibility and you never know... @JeffShavitz

_____
_____
_____

41

You never know who'll be helpful in your career so treat everyone with respect. Plus, it's the right thing to do. @JeffShavitz

_____
_____
_____

Section III: Authentic Relationships Matter

42

Remember the birthdays of those you connect with--you'll be surprised how far a birthday wish or simple gift goes. @JeffShavitz

_____
_____
_____

43

If you have been successful in servicing your customer, respectfully ask them to recommend you to others. @JeffShavitz

_____

_____

_____

44

Keeping in touch with past employees and employers is a great way to expand your network for the future. @JeffShavitz

_____

_____

_____

Section III: Authentic Relationships Matter

45

Think of a potential contact as your friend, not as a client, which makes it easier to cultivate a relationship. @JeffShavitz

46

Make eye contact when speaking with a person at a networking event. Do you do this naturally or do you need to work on it? @JeffShavitz

47

Try to link and connect other like-minded people--it will always come back to help you. @JeffShavitz

48

Have "insightful questions" ready to ask when meeting people for the first time. @JeffShavitz

Section IV: Get Connected

Section IV

Get Connected

Times have changed. Technologies and social media platforms evolve daily. You must remain with the times in order to effectively continue to cultivate your network. Networks, through the power of the Internet, are no longer local – the opportunity to develop relationships nationally and worldwide are just a click away.

Section IV: Get Connected

49

There's skill in using email to network--learn how to effectively communicate without turning it into junk e-mail. @JeffShavitz

50

Are you plugged in? I mean, REALLY plugged into all the different social media outlets? @JeffShavitz

51

Creating relevant articles to share through your blog is a great way to do social networking. @JeffShavitz

Section IV: Get Connected

52

Be strategic in how you network; w/ the Internet, you can learn about potential prospects prior to your 1st meeting. @JeffShavitz

_____

_____

_____

53

How can I network? Have you ever heard of social media? @JeffShavitz

Section IV: Get Connected

54

Get a LinkedIn profile, Facebook page, and a Twitter account to help build your circle of influence. @JeffShavitz

55

If you can't/won't write a handwritten note, an email version will suffice--don't be lazy. @JeffShavitz

56

Pick a Customer Relationship Management (CRM) that's best for your business--all have different benefits & work flow. @JeffShavitz

Section IV: Get Connected

57

Put your LinkedIn, Twitter, and Facebook links on your business card and in your email signature. @JeffShavitz

_____
_____
_____

58

Learn how LinkedIn works--take a course or hire a consultant to help build your network. Use the advanced features. @JeffShavitz

Section IV: Get Connected

59

Start building your powerful network of contacts from day 1 - do not wait until you really need those relationships! @JeffShavitz

___

___

___

60

Before you throw out your "junk mail," take an extra second to read it, as it may be more valuable than you think. @JeffShavitz

___

___

___

61

Testimonials on your website are a great way to increase your network and prospects for new customers. @JeffShavitz

62

LinkedIn is the ultimate business networking portal. Do you feel like you use it effectively? @JeffShavitz

63

Use a CRM tool and write a few personal things about the person (children's name, hobbies, birthday, etc.). @JeffShavitz

_____
_____
_____

64

Update your website and social media profiles every three months to keep your info current. @JeffShavitz

Section V: Keep in Mind

Section V

Keep in Mind

There are simple, important and powerful truths to create your networking plan. It's a strategy. It's not luck. These AhaMessages (e.g. axioms) will serve as your blueprint to networking success.

Section V: Keep in Mind

65

You must create a Networking Plan--just like you create an overall Business Plan. Put your plan in writing. @JeffShavitz

---

66

Filter your business cards monthly and evaluate the potential power of each respective relationship. @JeffShavitz

---

67

Set a yearly budget of what you will donate to charity; helps your finances when people contact you for philanthropy. @JeffShavitz

68

Develop your own tribe of loyal followers throughout your personal and professional career. @JeffShavitz

Section V: Keep in Mind

69

Remember to always follow up on any leads sent your way and report back the results. @JeffShavitz

_____
_____
_____

70

Always carry business cards in your wallet or pocketbook. Do you have them now?
@JeffShavitz

71

Buy a business card scanner & mobile app to download info into your CRM to keep your contacts & prospects organized.
@JeffShavitz

Section V: Keep in Mind

72

A "warm lead" definitely beats a "cold lead." Work hard to get referrals. @JeffShavitz

73

You must sincerely believe in your product and/or service to sell it to others--if you don't, find another company. @JeffShavitz

Section V: Keep in Mind

74

When in the car, listen to sales audio CDs/Podcasts vs. music to keep learning how to network & sell more effectively. @JeffShavitz

75

The most frustrating part of networking is deciding where to spend that time & maintaining patience with the process. @JeffShavitz

76

Understand there is a degree of risk when a fellow entrepreneur provides you with an introduction to their network. @JeffShavitz

Section V: Keep in Mind

77

A relationship could be jeopardized if the hand-off of a networking referral goes poorly. @JeffShavitz

78

Don't expect to receive 20 leads the day after your first networking event. It doesn't happen that way. @JeffShavitz

79

The "law of reciprocity" always works: where people instinctively want to help others who have helped them in the past. @JeffShavitz

_____
_____
_____

Section V: Keep in Mind

80

Shockingly, many people never call a prospect within 2 days to introduce themselves. After that, it's too late! @JeffShavitz

_____
_____
_____

81

Anybody in the inner circle of my network is a direct reflection of me. @JeffShavitz

_____
_____
_____

82

The feeling of being "uncomfortable" is a good thing at a networking event. Push yourself to meet new people.
@JeffShavitz

_____
_____
_____

Section V: Keep in Mind

83

Your competitors can and will be very important to your network. Are you networking with any of them? @JeffShavitz

84

Customers have a hard time finding great vendors. Introductions are very powerful. @JeffShavitz

85

Clients prefer an average product from an extraordinary company than an extraordinary product from a bad company. @JeffShavitz

86

Said differently, there are many similar products on the market, but there is only one you--sell yourself! @JeffShavitz

Section V: Keep in Mind

87

Network at industry tradeshows. I don't view my competitors as the enemy, I view them as my contemporaries. @JeffShavitz

88

No excuses--there are more networking possibilities than ever before. @JeffShavitz

89

Using email properly is a great way to connect with people. @JeffShavitz

Section V: Keep in Mind

90

You can never collect too many business cards--whether at dinner parties, conferences, or at other meetings. @JeffShavitz

91

Holiday time is a great time to connect with your network. @JeffShavitz

92

You're not exploiting relationships for personal gain, but introducing others to your products for their gain. @JeffShavitz

Section V: Keep in Mind

93

Question for you, "Do you own one good navy blue or black suit?" Male or female, the answer should be yes. @JeffShavitz

94

Say a new person's name when you meet them. Use a game to remember all the names. Try it! Does it help? @JeffShavitz

95

I recommend Dale Carnegie's 1936 book, "How to Win Friends & Influence People," which has sold more than 15M copies. @JeffShavitz

Section V: Keep in Mind

96

Introducing 2 superconnectors together is easy: they'll take it from there & be forever grateful for the intro. @JeffShavitz

97

Don't always jump right into business questions: start with casual conversion--but not, "How's the weather?" @JeffShavitz

_____
_____
_____

Section V: Keep in Mind

98

Do you have a 30-second elevator pitch about your business you can recite without stuttering? @JeffShavitz

99

With so many commoditized products and services on the market, what really differentiates them is YOU! @JeffShavitz

100

Forming strategic partners is a powerful way to leverage your relationships. @JeffShavitz

_____

_____

_____

Section V: Keep in Mind

101

Presentation & professionalism count when networking. First appearances are critical to developing relationships. @JeffShavitz

102

Public speaking is a powerful way to meet many people quickly. Public speaking is scary until you do it several times. @JeffShavitz

103

Two of my best friends are direct competitors. We share our relationships to learn and grow. Do you do this? You should. @JeffShavitz

104

Networking done properly is one of the best ways to grow your company and your bottom-line profitability. @JeffShavitz

Section VI: Your RoadMap to Success

Section VI

Your RoadMap to Success

Final set of AhaMessages to ponder. This AhaBook will get you started and help you continue your networking journey. It is absolutely essential to make friends, do favors, and have others feel that they matter to you.

Section VI: Your RoadMap to Success

105

People who enjoy networking in a positive way seem to have the greatest returns. @JeffShavitz

106

One key contact can change the future of your company--forever. Did you meet that contact this week? @JeffShavitz

107

A great networking event opening line: "If there's anything I can do to help you w/ potential leads, let me know." @JeffShavitz

108

If I offer a connection, I want to ensure that the person will follow up quickly, which reflects positively on me. @JeffShavitz

Section VI: Your RoadMap to Success

109

We are always selling in some way; what's interesting is that most people don't get this core business philosophy. @JeffShavitz

110

The Golden Rule really prevails: "It's better to give than receive." Are you truly following this rule? @JeffShavitz

111

Everyone talks about networking w/ the outside world--how are your internal networking skills with fellow employees? @JeffShavitz

_____
_____
_____

Section VI: Your RoadMap to Success

112

Women: going to the bathroom at a networking event is a great way to meet other women--sounds weird, but it works. @JeffShavitz

113

Stop talking and listen--I know it's very hard to do! @JeffShavitz

114

Say a quick hello on the airplane to the person sitting next to you. You never know, it could be a great contact. @JeffShavitz

Section VI: Your RoadMap to Success

115

Cold calling, put in basic English, "sucks." There are much better ways to meet quality people. @JeffShavitz

116

Networking w/ face-to-face communication is more meaningful & memorable than building a relationship online. @JeffShavitz

117

Did you ever think of getting into
a network marketing business?
It could be just right for you. @JeffShavitz

Section VI: Your RoadMap to Success

118

Can you think of someone right now who you can help with their career path? If so, share the connection. @JeffShavitz

_____
_____
_____

119

Superconnectors are people who connect others--it's a powerful skill worth cultivating. @JeffShavitz

120

Ask quality questions. And actually listen to the answer. @JeffShavitz

Section VI: Your RoadMap to Success

121

How much money do you want to earn this year? Work backward through key contacts you'll need to accomplish this goal. @JeffShavitz

_____
_____
_____

122

When you think of "networking," take the word "working" out of your vocabulary--it shouldn't be work! @JeffShavitz

123

Cool eyeglasses can make you look really smart--even if you "fake it" and put in clear lenses. @JeffShavitz

Section VI: Your RoadMap to Success

124

6 degrees of separation is the theory that we are 6 or fewer introductions from any other person in the world. @JeffShavitz

125

Networking can help you land your dream job or meet that dream prospect. @JeffShavitz

126

You don't have to be a social person; just a smart one. @JeffShavitz

Section VI: Your RoadMap to Success

127

An event that seems like a waste of time could easily lead to new business six months from now. Don't be downtrodden. @JeffShavitz

_____
_____
_____

128

"Instant networking" to meet quality people is a myth. Would you introduce contacts if you didn't know the person? @JeffShavitz

Section VI: Your RoadMap to Success

129

At the end of the day, it's your "Rolodex" of trusted relationships that is the greatest asset in your life. @JeffShavitz

130

The currency of real networking is not greed, but generosity.
--Keith @Ferrazzi via @JeffShavitz

131

Have fun with networking--it's a gift to meet new people. @JeffShavitz

132

It's wonderful to have friends in your industry to share war stories and advice about current and future trends. @JeffShavitz

Section VI: Your RoadMap to Success

133

Read and share "The Power of Residual Income" by Jeff Shavitz.
http://aha.pub/residualincome
@JeffShavitz

134

Networking is not hard--if you can't do it, it's most likely your fault. @JeffShavitz

135

It's critical to have a network of trusted advisors who surround you to help with key decisions. @JeffShavitz

Section VI: Your RoadMap to Success

136

It's important to have over 500 "friends" on LinkedIn, or it seems like you don't know a lot of people. @JeffShavitz

137

I am a big proponent of the written thank you note--it's a lost art of communication. @JeffShavitz

138

Using technology, staying in touch, and meeting new potential contacts is so easy compared to just 10 years ago. @JeffShavitz

Section VI: Your RoadMap to Success

139

You can never attend too many conferences. A day out of the office is a day to grow your relationships. @JeffShavitz

_____
_____
_____

140

Some of your best friends start off as business relationships. @JeffShavitz

About the Author

Jeff Shavitz is a successful entrepreneur. He worked as an investment banker at Lehman Brothers in the Corporate Finance/Mergers and Acquisitions Group, specializing in transactions ranging from $250MM–$500MM. With an offer in hand to attend graduate school to earn his MBA and continue his climb up the corporate ladder, Jeff consciously decided to leave this fast-paced, well-paying position to start up a one-person business. Friends said, "What is he thinking?"

A passion for creating "a life of his own" was the driving force in determining Jeff's business future. Out of his New York apartment, while still working on Wall Street, he created "Spectoculars," a branded paper-folding binocular that received an NFL license in 1991. At Super Bowl XXX, 250,000 pairs were distributed.

Fast-forward several years and Jeff cofounded Charge Card Systems Inc., a national credit card processing company that helps merchants with their processing requirements, including the acceptance of Visa, MasterCard, American Express, and Discover. The company grew to more than 700 sales agents throughout the country with three regional offices. In 2012, Jeff and his partners sold the business to Card Connect, owned by private equity firm FTV Capital. The purchase was the company's largest acquisition to date.

The culmination of Jeff's past experiences with the small and mid-size business owners is TrafficJamming LLC (www.trafficjamming.com), a membership association for business owners and entrepreneurs. All businesses want more traffic—in essence, traffic means sales. TrafficJamming provides its members with a destination website filled with information, technology tools, and insights to help grow your business. TrafficJamming is not a buying club or traditional business group, but rather a modern organization to help executives realize their professional dreams. Among its many services, TrafficJamming provides proven and cutting-edge technology solutions to help build awareness of our members' products and services—with the ultimate goal of building a loyal tribe of clients.

In addition to *Jeff Shavitz on Networking: Get Connected*, Jeff has also published the following books:

– *Size Doesn't Matter: Why Small Business Is BIG Business*, which hit #1 on the Amazon new releases in Entrepreneurship. In this book, Jeff details his personal and professional experiences, observations, challenges, and rewards in operating small businesses.

– *Jeff Shavitz on Small Business AhaMessages™: 140 Key Axioms That Every Business Owner Should Consider*, a collection of 140 key axioms that every business owner should consider when starting or running their companies.

– *Jeff Shavitz on The Power of Residual Income: You Can Bank On It*, a collection of 140 AhaMessages that educate business owners on the power of residual and recurring income versus transactional income.

Jeff received his Bachelor of Arts degree in Economics from Tufts University and spent one semester at the London School of Economics, specializing in finance. He is very active in numerous charitable and civic community organizations and business groups, including Young Presidents' Organization.

He is married and has two daughters, a son, and two dogs. Besides being with family, enjoying good health, and living to see worldwide peace, Jeff's selfish goal is to play the 100 top golf courses in the United States.

To learn more about the author, visit www.JeffShavitz.com or contact him at jeff@trafficjamming.com or 800-878-4100.

Amplifier™
Democratizing Thought Leadership

The Aha Amplifier™ is the only thought leadership platform with a built in marketplace making it easy to share curated content from like-minded thought leaders. There are over 25k diverse AhaMessages™ from thought leaders from around the world.

The Aha Amplifier makes it easy to create, organize and share your own thought leadership AhaMessages in digestible, bite-sized morsels. Users are able to democratize thought leadership in their organizations by: 1) Making it easy for any advocate to share existing content with their Twitter, Facebook, LinkedIn & Google+ networks. 2) Allowing internal experts to create their own thought leadership content, and 3) Encouraging the expert's advocates to share that content on their networks.

The experience of many authors is that they have been able to create their social media enabled AhaBooks™ of 140 AhaMessages in less than a day.

Sign up for a free account at
http://www.AhaAmplifier.com today!

Please pick up a copy of this book in the Aha Amplifier and share each AhaMessage socially at
http://aha.pub/jeffshavitznetworking.

www.ingramcontent.com/pod-product-compliance
Ingram Content Group UK Ltd.
Pitfield, Milton Keynes, MK11 3LW, UK
UKHW021253180426
11947UKWH00010B/760